PINE HILL MIDDLE SCHOOL
LIBRARY

Careers without College

Actor

by Kathryn A. Quinlan

Content Consultant:
William Schill
Talent Agent
William Schill Agency, Inc.

CAPSTONE
HIGH/LOW BOOKS
an imprint of Capstone Press

CAPSTONE PRESS
818 North Willow Street • Mankato, Minnesota 56001
http://www.capstone-press.com

Copyright © 1998 Capstone Press. All rights reserved.
No part of this book may be reproduced without written permission from the publisher.
The publisher takes no responsibility for the use of any of the materials
or methods described in this book, nor for the products thereof.
Printed in the United States of America.

Library of Congress Cataloging-in-Publication Data
Quinlan, Kathryn A.
    Actor/Kathryn A. Quinlan.
       p. cm.--(Careers without college)
    Includes bibliographical references and index.
    ISBN 1-56065-699-9
    1. Acting--Vocational guidance--Juvenile literature.
    I. Title. II. Series: Careers without college (Mankato, Minn.)
PN2055.Q56 1998
792'.028'023--DC21

97-35228
CIP
AC

Photo Credits:
International Stock/Kennon Cooke, 22; Dusty Willison, 20
New York State Theatre Institute, 25; Timothy H. Raab, 4, 6, 9, 12, 14, 32, 39,
    41; Fred Ricard, cover
Photo Network/Chad Ehlers, 44; Michael Philip Manheim, 11
Unicorn Stock Photos/ChromoSohm/Sohm, 19
Valan Photos/Kennon Cooke, 27, 28, 30; John Eastcott and Yva Momatiuk,
    35, 36; John Fowler, 17

Table of Contents

Fast Facts 5

Chapter 1   What Actors Do 7

Chapter 2   What the Job Is Like 15

Chapter 3   Training to Be an Actor 23

Chapter 4   Salary and Job Outlook 31

Chapter 5   Where the Job Can Lead 37

Words to Know 42

To Learn More 45

Useful Addresses 46

Internet Sites 47

Index 48

Fast Facts

Career Title — Actor

Minimum Educational Requirement — High school diploma

Certification Requirement — None

U.S. Salary Range — $5,000 to more than $1,000,000

Canadian Salary Range — $7,300 to more than $1,000,000 (Canadian dollars)

U.S. Job Outlook — Much faster than the average

Canadian Job Outlook — Much faster than the average

DOT Cluster — Professional, technical, and managerial occupations
(Dictionary of Occupational Titles)

DOT Number — 150.047-010

GOE Number — 01.03.02
(Guide for Occupational Exploration)

NOC — 5113
(National Occupational Classification—Canada)

Chapter 1

What Actors Do

Actors play parts in movies, plays, television shows, and radio shows. They pretend to be different characters. A character is the part an actor plays in a play, movie, or show. Actors try to speak and move like the characters they play.

Rehearsing and Performing

Actors must learn their lines. Lines are words actors say as characters. Many actors sing and

Many actors sing and dance.

dance. They must learn the words and music to songs. They must also learn dance steps.

Actors rehearse together after they learn their lines and dance steps. Rehearse means to practice many times. Actors who dance spend many hours rehearsing their dance steps.

Directors often ask actors to try new ways of acting while they rehearse. A director is the person who is in charge of a show. Directors help actors act with one another. Directors help actors decide how to say their lines. They show actors where to stand and how to move.

Actors perform after they rehearse. Some actors perform in the same show many times. A show can be a play, musical, movie, or television program. Actors work hard to do a good job each time. Other actors perform in new shows every week or even every day. They must learn new lines quickly.

Finding Jobs

Actors spend a lot of time looking for jobs. There are more actors than acting jobs. Actors learn about

Many actors must learn the words and music to songs.

new jobs in many ways. They talk to other actors. They read newspapers. Many actors also work with agents. An agent is someone who helps actors find work. Actors pay agents for their help.

Actors read scripts to learn about parts they want to play. A script is the story for a play, movie, or television show. Actors try to understand the stories and the characters. Then they audition for parts. Audition means to try out for a part. Actors audition for the people who plan shows. These people pick the best actor for each part.

Kinds of Acting

Actors act in many kinds of shows. Some act in comedies. A comedy is a show that makes people laugh. Other actors work in musicals. A musical is a show with singing and dancing. Actors in musicals must be able to act, sing, and dance. Some actors work in operas. An opera is a play in which actors sing all the words. Actors in operas must have good voices.

An opera is a play in which actors sing all the words.

Some people think acting looks easy. But acting is hard work. Good actors make acting look easy. Actors must learn many lines. They must show audiences how characters think and feel. An audience is people who watch or listen to a play, movie, or show. Actors sometimes do risky things like jump off buildings.

Actors work many hours. Most actors work at night and on weekends. Many also work on holidays. Only a small number of actors become famous or wealthy. Most actors work extra jobs to earn enough money. People who decide to work as actors must enjoy acting.

Most actors enjoy their work. They believe acting is a good way to share ideas with other people. Actors like helping people think about things in new ways. They also like helping people have fun.

Actors must show audiences how characters think and feel.

Chapter 2

What the Job Is Like

There are acting jobs in most cities in the United States and Canada. However, many paying jobs in acting are in large cities. Many actors find paying acting jobs in New York and Los Angeles. Actors in Canada find paying acting jobs in big cities such as Toronto. There are also acting jobs in some small Canadian towns. Many actors work at the Shakespeare Theater Festival

There are acting jobs in most cities in the United States and Canada.

in Stratford, Ontario. A theater is a place where actors perform plays, musicals, and operas. Other actors act at the Shaw Festival in Niagara on the Lake, Ontario.

Places Actors Work

Actors work in many different places. Theme parks such as Disney World hire actors to play Disney characters and to sing and dance. Some actors work in theaters. Others work in studios. A studio is a place where movies, television shows, and radio shows are made.

Sometimes actors must travel. Actors often perform the same play in many cities. They may live in one city for months while performing their plays. Actors move when their plays move to other cities.

Some movies take place in unusual settings. Actors often travel to places such as mountains and jungles to make television shows and movies. Actors call this working on location.

Actors must often work on location.

Plays and Movies

Every acting job is different. Acting in plays is different from acting in movies, television shows, and radio shows. Actors perform plays in front of audiences. Actors must perform a whole play at one time. They cannot start over if they make mistakes or forget lines. Actors rehearse plays for many weeks before performing for audiences.

Directors film movies in small parts called scenes. Directors rarely film scenes in front of audiences. Movie actors rehearse each scene several times. Then the director films the scenes.

Movie directors may film one scene many times. Each filmed scene is a take. Directors choose the best takes for their movies. Some movies take months to film. Movie actors play the same characters throughout this time.

Television and Radio Shows

Directors film television shows in small scenes. Like movie directors, television directors may

---

Directors film movies in small parts called scenes.

also film many takes of each scene. Many television actors cannot spend much time rehearsing. They act in many shows each year. They often learn new scripts each week. Some television actors play characters in soap operas. A soap opera is a television series that has a new show every weekday. Soap opera actors must learn new lines every day.

Some actors perform live radio shows. Other actors record their shows. Audiences do not see radio programs. Radio actors must use their voices to help audiences understand characters.

Soap opera actors must learn new lines every day.

Chapter 3

Training to Be an Actor

Actors do not need college degrees. But most actors have some kind of formal training. Some people study acting in college. Others take classes at acting schools. Many people who want to be actors also study singing and dancing.

Actors work as often as they can get parts. They may act in small theaters. They may act in

Sometimes actors work as extras.

small parts in television shows or movies. Sometimes actors work as extras. An extra is an actor who plays a minor part. Extras rarely have speaking parts. Directors hire extras to make scenes seem more like real life. Many actors work as extras to get acting practice and to earn money.

Some actors join unions. A union is a group that seeks fair treatment and better pay for workers. Sometimes actors must belong to unions before they can work. For example, actors who act in Broadway plays must belong to the Actors' Equity Association. Broadway is a street in New York City with many theaters. There are acting unions for many different kinds of actors.

Exploring This Career

Actors do many things to get ready for their careers. Young actors often perform in school

Young actors may build sets and props.

plays. They may build sets. A set is the stage and setting for a play, movie, or show. A set may include a film location or a stage and its scenery. Actors may also build props. A prop is anything an actor uses or carries in a play.

English classes are also a good way to prepare for a career in acting. English classes help actors understand the meanings of stories and plays. This can help actors understand how characters think and feel.

Speech classes are also important. They offer training and practice in public speaking. Actors must be able to speak in front of people. They must be able to make people laugh or cry.

Learning to sing and dance can also be valuable. Many high schools and colleges offer singing and dancing classes. Private lessons are another way to learn how to sing or dance.

Attending plays can also be useful. Young actors can learn by watching what other actors do.

Actors must be able to make people laugh or cry.

Qualities of Good Actors

People who are afraid to fail should not become actors. Actors audition for more parts than they get. Some actors receive bad comments about their performances. Audiences do not always like the way actors perform. Actors must be willing to learn from their experiences. They must be brave enough to try new things.

Actors must be willing to work unusual hours. Many actors work at night or on weekends. Actors need to follow directions and work well with other people.

Actors must be brave enough to try new things.

Chapter 4

Salary and Job Outlook

The amount of money actors make from acting depends on many things. Famous actors can earn large amounts of money. But most actors do not earn enough to pay their bills. Most actors must work other jobs to make the additional money they need. Some actors work as waiters, bartenders, or taxi drivers. They work these jobs when they are not going on

Some actors work as waiters, bartenders, or taxi drivers.

31

auditions or acting in shows. They may have to give up their jobs if they get a part in a show.

Earnings

Actors receive different amounts for different kinds of acting. Many movie and television actors earn more than actors in plays. Most actors with important roles get paid more than actors who have small parts. Actors with experience earn more than new actors. Famous actors earn more than unknown actors.

In the United States, Broadway actors earn about $975 per week. Actors who work in small theaters may earn from $355 to $609 per week. Actors who work as extras earn about $99 per day. The amount actors earn can depend on union rules. Many actors make money every time movies or television shows are rerun. Earnings for reruns are residuals.

In the United States, Broadway actors earn about $975 per week.

Canadian actors also earn different amounts of money for different kinds of jobs. Canadian actors earn an average of $34,800 per year for full-time work.

Acting is a growing job field in the United States and Canada. There are many acting jobs. But there will always be more actors than acting jobs. It takes talent, hard work, and some luck to succeed as an actor.

It takes talent, hard work, and some luck to succeed as an actor.

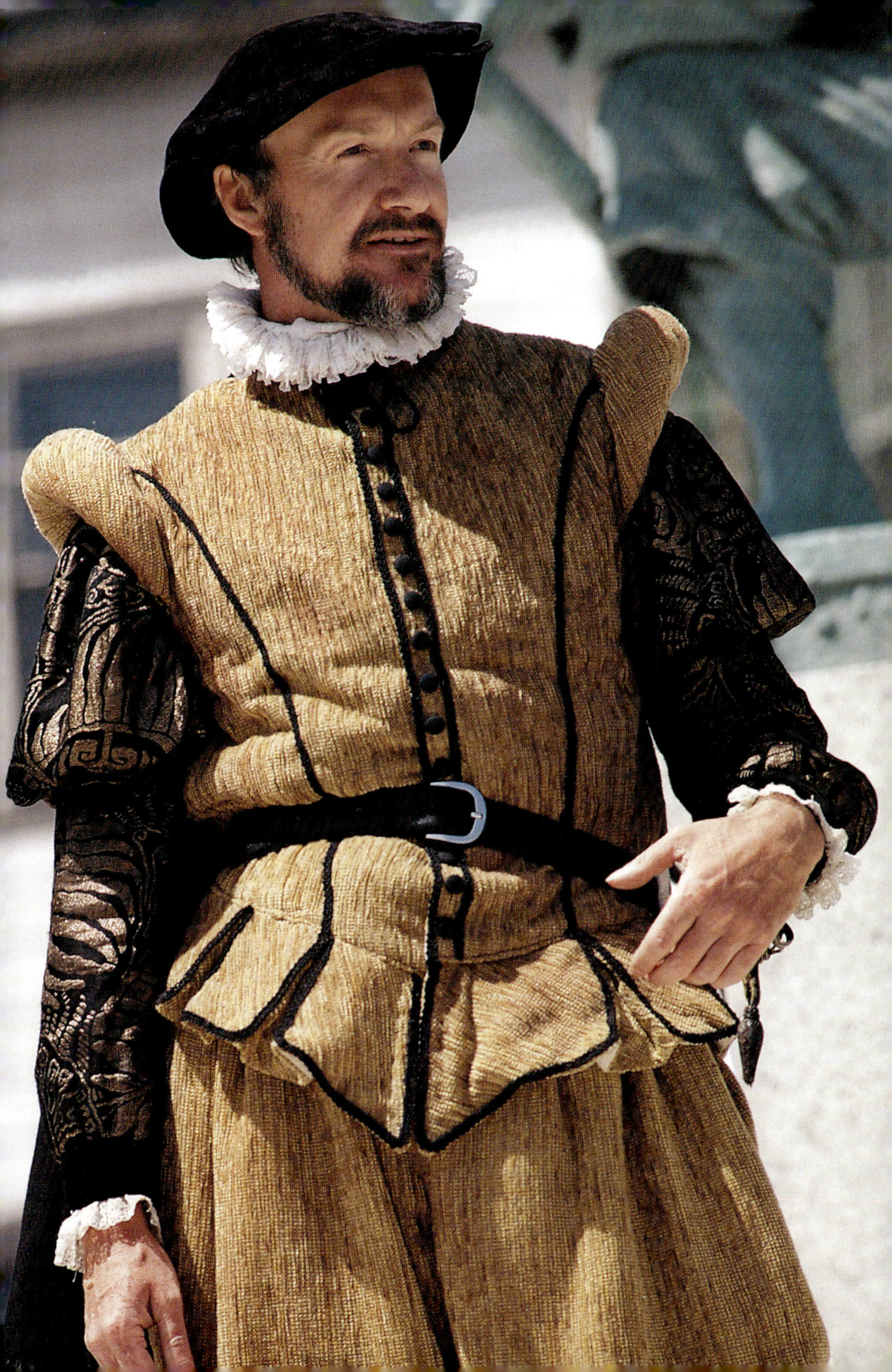

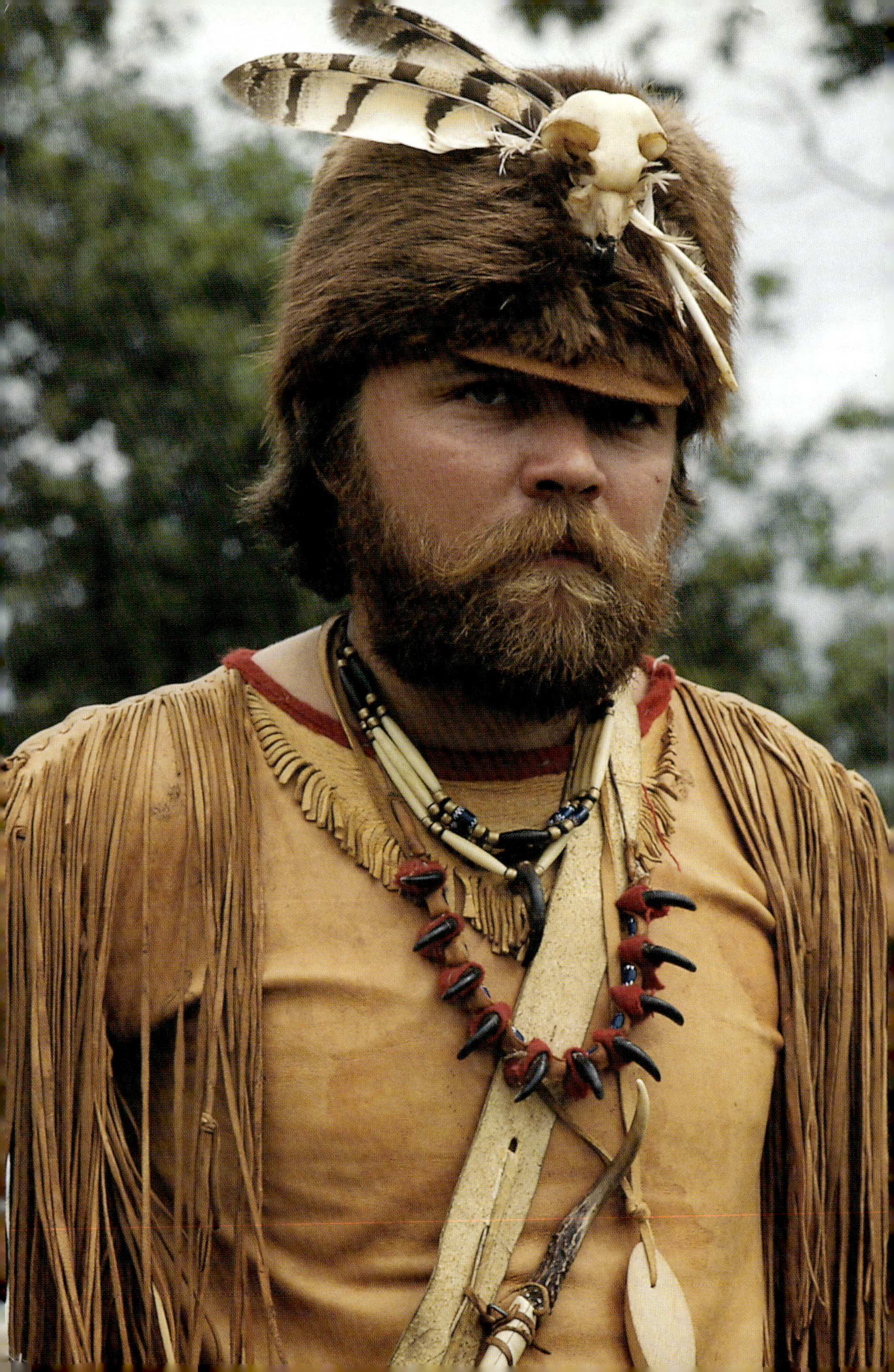

Chapter 5

Where the Job Can Lead

Actors often start their acting careers by taking small parts. They take any parts that will give them practice and experience. They take parts that will show directors their talents. Talent is a natural ability or skill. Then actors audition for bigger, more important parts. Talented actors may play the main roles in plays, movies, or shows. But they often have to work for a long time first.

Actors often start their acting careers by taking small parts.

Television

Television actors may start by acting in commercials. Commercials are television or radio ads. Television actors may receive small speaking parts. Later, they may earn parts as main characters.

Some television actors begin by acting in soap operas. Actors who do well may earn roles in prime time programs. Prime time programs have larger audiences. Actors who appear in these programs often earn more money.

Theater and Movies

Theater actors may start out acting in small cities. They try to get big roles in these cities. Then they might audition for small parts in large cities. After many years, they may play leading roles in big cities.

Movie actors often start out as extras or in small roles. Directors may allow actors who have talent

Theater actors may play leading roles after working for many years.

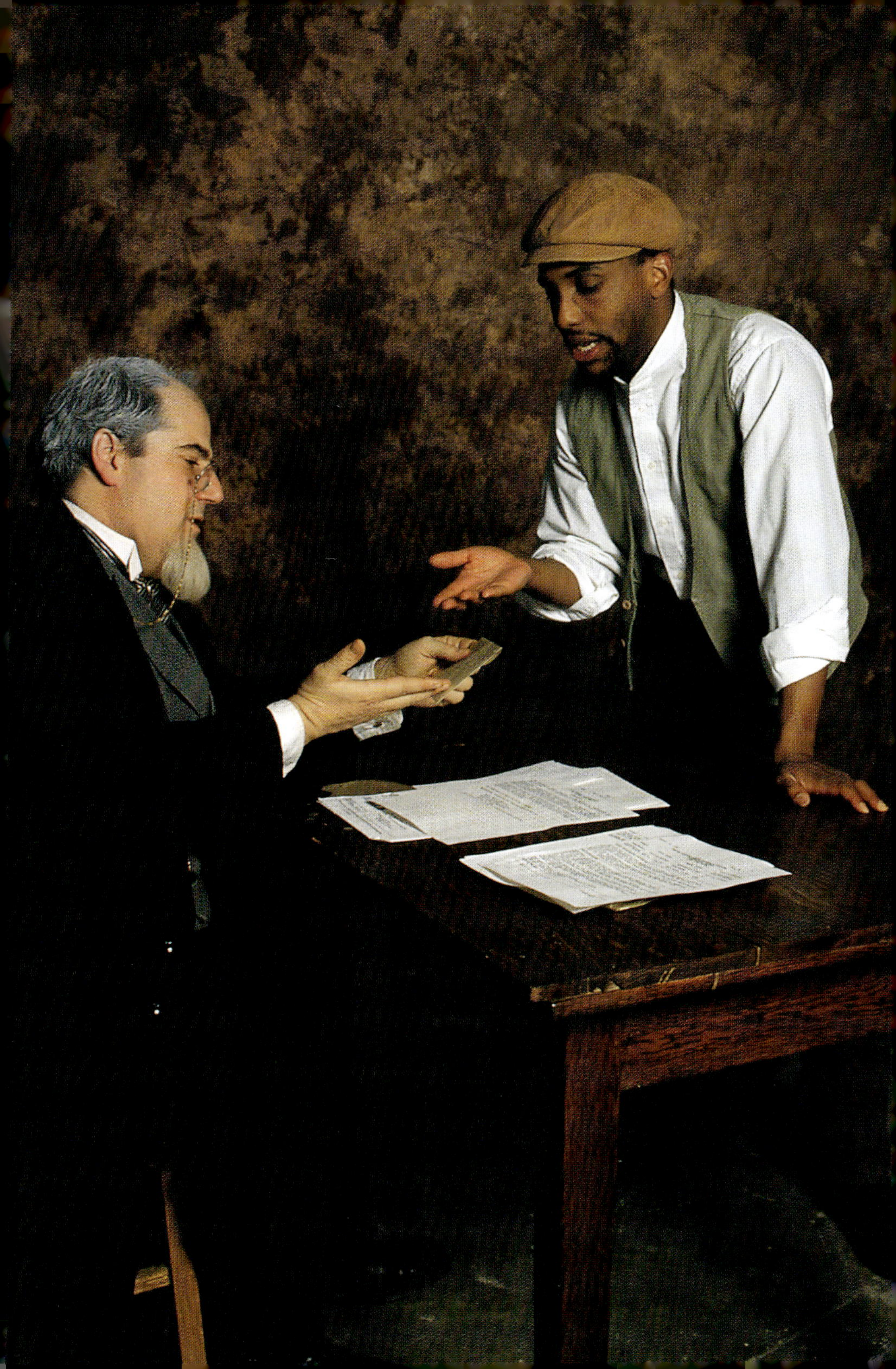

to play larger, more important parts. Some actors eventually become famous. They often star in movies.

Related Jobs

Some actors move to other jobs related to acting. Some become directors. Others become acting teachers. Actors may decide to write scripts. Some actors use their talents to become television or radio announcers.

It is difficult to make a living as an actor. Even good actors do not always get the parts they want. But thousands of people choose to be actors each year.

Most people become actors because they love acting. They do not mind working for little pay. Actors enjoy entertaining audiences. They also enjoy learning about characters and trying new roles.

Most people become actors because they love acting.

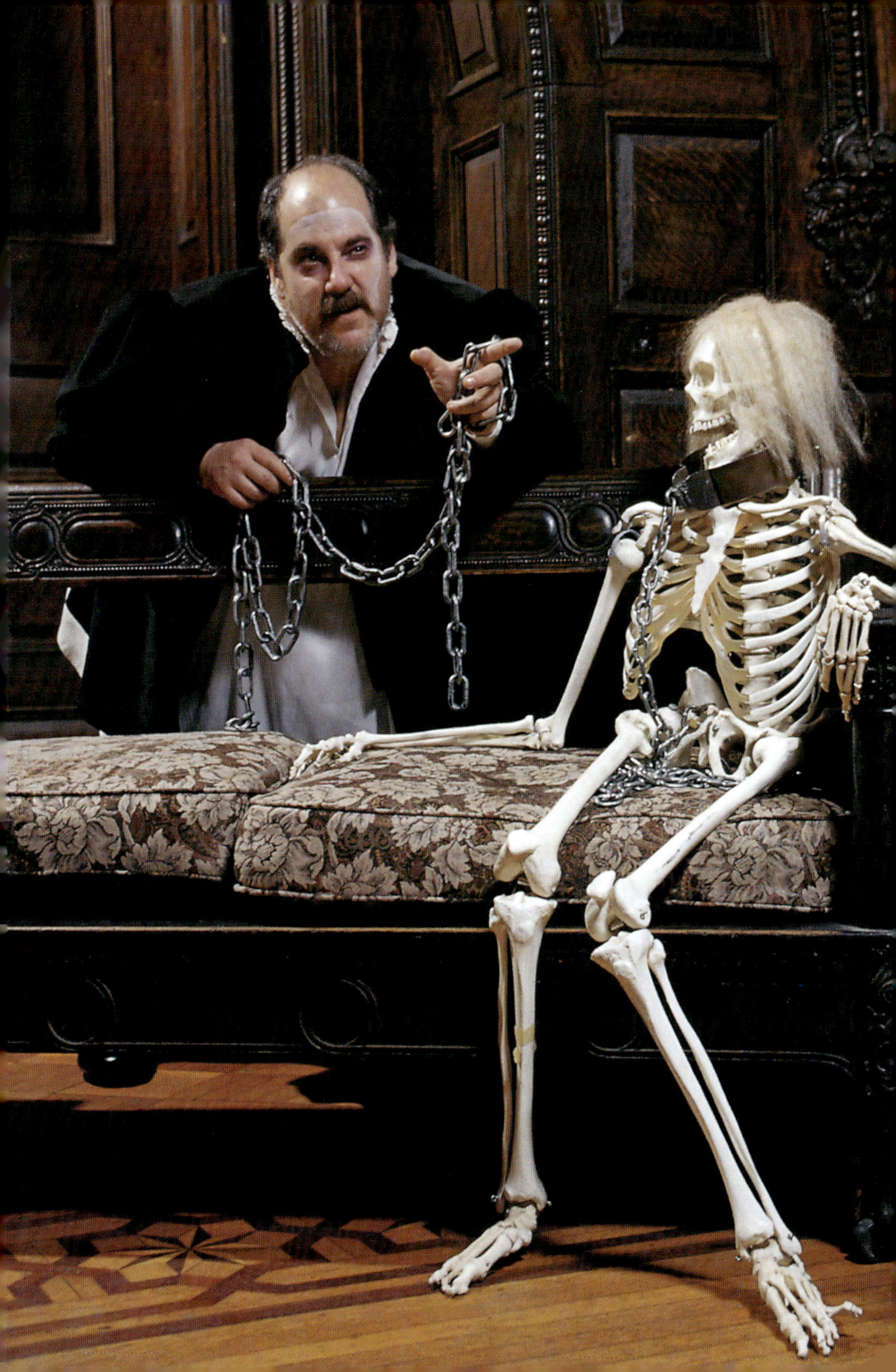

Words to Know

agent (AY-juhnt)—someone who helps actors find work

audience (AW-dee-uhnss)—people who watch or listen to a play, movie, or show

audition (aw-DISH-uhn)—to try out for a part

character (KA-rik-tur)—the part an actor plays in a play, movie, or show

comedy (KOM-uh-dee)—a show that makes people laugh

director (duh-REK-tur)—the person who is in charge of a show

extra (EK-struh)—an actor who plays a minor part

lines (LINES)—words actors say as characters

musical (MYOO-zuh-kuhl)—a show with singing and dancing
opera (OP-ur-uh)—a play in which actors sing all the words
script (SKRIPT)—the story for a play, movie, or television show
soap opera (SOHP OP-ur-uh)—a television series that has a new show every weekday
studio (STOO-dee-oh)—a place where movies, television shows, and radio shows are made
take (TAYK)—a filmed scene
theater (THEE-uh-tur)—a place where actors perform plays
union (YOON-yuhn)—a group that seeks fair treatment and better pay for workers

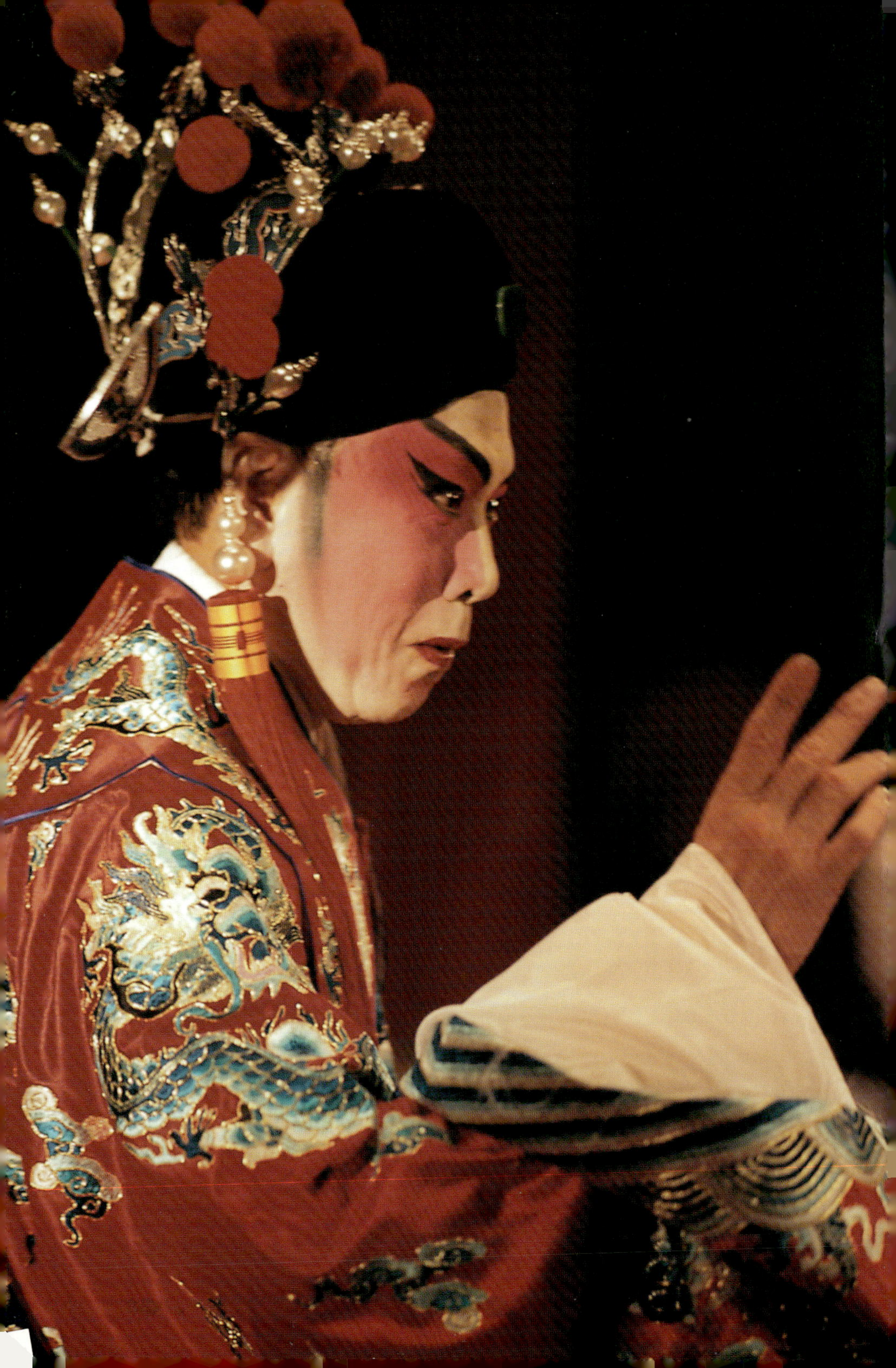

To Learn More

Bulloch, Ivan and Diane James. *I Want to Be an Actor.* Chicago: World Book, 1996.

Conlon, Laura. *Actors.* Vero Beach, Fla.: Rourke Press, 1994.

Greenspon, Jaq. *Acting.* Lincolnwood, Ill.: VGM Career Horizons, 1996.

Lantz, Francess. *Be a Star!* Mahweh, N.J.: Rainbow Bridge, 1996.

Weeks, Jessica Vitkus. *Television.* New York: Crestwood House, 1994.

Useful Addresses

Canadian Actor's Equity Association
260 Richmond Street East
Toronto, Ontario M5A 1P4
Canada

New York State Theatre Institute
155 River Street
Troy, NY 12180

Screen Actors Guild
7065 Hollywood Boulevard
Hollywood, CA 90028

Internet Sites

Actors, Directors, and Producers
http://stats.bls.gov/oco/ocos093.htm

American Federation of Television and Radio Artists
http://www.aftra.org/home.html

NYS Theatre Institute
http://www.crisny.org/not-for-profit/nysti

Screen Actors Guild
http://www.sag.com/

Index

acting school, 23
agent, 10
announcer, 40
audition, 10, 29, 33, 37, 38

Broadway, 24, 33

comedy, 10

director, 8, 18, 24, 37, 40
Disney World, 16

earnings, 33-34
extra, 24, 33, 38

movie, 7, 8, 10, 13, 16, 18, 24, 26, 33, 37, 38-40
musical, 10

opera, 10

prop, 26

radio, 7, 16, 18-21, 38, 40
rehearse, 8, 18

scene, 18, 21, 24
script, 10, 21, 40
Shakespeare Theater Festival, 15
Shaw Festival, 16
soap opera, 21, 38

television, 7, 16, 18-21, 24, 33, 38, 40

union, 24, 33